Photographic Review: A Journal Devoted To Photography, Volume 23, Issue 4

Anonymous

PHOTOGRAPHIC REVIEW

Vol. 23   APRIL, 1917.   No. 4.

PHOTOGRAPHING MOTOR CARS AND MACHINERY.

Engineers are very exacting people to work for. They are trained to precision, and they expect those who work for them to be as accurate and as painstaking as they are themselves. Unless you appreciate this thoroughly, you will be wasting your time in attempting photographic work for engineering firms.

An engineer wants clear, sharp photographs with all the detail plainly shown. He expects you to set aside all your ideas of picture-making. Broad masses of shadow where the detail is suppressed will only irritate him. He wants photographs that will help a prospective customer to visualize a motor car, an engine, or a piece of machinery. A little cam, a spindle or a worm-screw will not seem important to the layman, but it may be a new invention, and in the eyes of the engineer the most important part of the machine. Your photograph must back up his specifications.

Motor cars are less difficult to photograph than machinery. They are portable, and it is therefore easy to get them placed in the best light and with the most suitable background. This, of course, refers only to finished cars. When engines or other separate parts have to be photographed, they require the same treatment as machinery.

Before you photograph a motor car, get to know in what respects it differs from other motor cars. Find out its selling points, because you may be pretty certain that the maker will want them shown to the best advantage. You should also ask whether the photographs are to be used for general advertising or for catalogue illustration. If they are wanted for general advertising, you can make them more telling by taking them on an open country road with a good stretch of scenery for a background. If they are wanted for catalogue illustrations, a plain background is best.

This work nearly always needs blocking out. Choose a grey day or work in a shady place. The polished surfaces will give you endless trouble if you attempt to photograph in sunlight. A Panchromatic Plate and a "K" Filter are necessary. Without them your color values will be ridiculous, and the photographs will probably be thrown back on your hands. Above all, use a long-focus lens—the longer the better. If you attempt the work with a wide angle lens in a confined space, you will get distortion, and remember, distortion worries an engineer more than it does most people.

Machinery is a tough problem. Small machines or, separate parts of large ones are easy enough to deal with. They can be placed on a bench or table in a good light. You will find, however, that most of your photographs will have to be taken when the machines are fitted up in their working positions. Here, as a rule, you have a poor light, a confined space for working, and an object with some parts shining like so many mirrors and other parts painted a deep green, red, grey or black.

Generally you can do a great deal towards reducing the harshness of the light by a liberal use of a cheap material like cheese cloth. Light softeners, however, must be used in the right way, otherwise they are worse than useless. Suppose, for instance, that you have to photograph a machine in a room where there is only one small window. Unless you have had experience, you will probably tack muslin over the window and imagine you have done all you can do to soften the light. As a matter of fact, you will have done little or nothing towards reducing the contrasts. You will have made it necessary to give a longer exposure, but that is about all. The way to go to work is to use the muslin exactly as you use a head screen in the studio. Hang it up between the machine and the window, as near the machine as you can without letting it show in the photograph. This allows all the light to come into the room, and softens only that which falls directly on the machine. There is as much reflected light as before, and so your shadow detail is not lost.

In addition to softening the light, much can be done to reduce contrasts by toning down the polished surfaces and lighting up the dark parts of the machine itself. You can do this, of course, only when you have the engineer's permission. As a rule, he is only too pleased to help you in any way, in fact, he will often go to the expense of having a machine specially painted when the advantages of this are pointed out to him beforehand.

There are two very good "non-shine" paints, both of which can be removed easily with turps when the photographs have been taken. The first is made by mixing equal parts of fine cement and stone dust with linseed oil to the consistency of ordinary paint. The second, which is easier to apply, should be used when there is much metal to cover. It is made by thinning white lead with turpentine to the consistency of cream and then adding a little lamp black, just enough to dull the white. To five parts of this mixture, one part of gold size should be added to make it stick.

When painting cannot be done, you can reduce the contrasts by daubing the bright parts with putty. The dark painted parts may also be daubed with putty and then dusted with powdered chalk.

The floor of a machine room is generally dark and oil-stained. It will help the shadows if you cover the floor with newspapers, under the machine, and round it to a distance of four or five feet.

Another useful dodge for picking up the shadow detail is to use a mirror for reflecting light into the dark corners. The mirror can be held in the hand while the exposure is being made, and the light directed to bits of detail which are half hidden in the shadows.

When a machine is lighted from two sides, it is best to block out one of the windows. Cross lights destroy the relief in the rounded parts. They give double high lights and confuse the detail.

The most trying subject of all is a machine which has to be photographed against the light. The best way out of the difficulty is to block up the window, or wait until night, and then make your exposure by flashlight, preferably a magnesium blow lamp. There are occasions, however, when the photographs must be taken by daylight, and when you are compelled to make the best of what light there is. In cases of this kind a mirror is very useful for reflecting light back to the dark side of the machine.

The background in a machine room is usually a confused mass of belts, shaftings and other gear. Unless you hang up a white sheet behind your subject, you will find great difficulty in picking out its various parts when you come to block out the negative.

With regard to exposure and development, you will find that the best results are secured by giving a very long exposure—one that would in ordinary work amount to excessive over exposure—and by developing with half, or less, the normal quantity of carbonate of soda in the developer.

Blocking out on the negative must be done very carefully. This is not an easy task where there are many intricate parts to contend with. Opaque is a good substance to use. It is easy to put on and it does not peel off when dry, as so often happens with India ink. To get clean edges you must go over the outlines with a ruling pen. And be careful not to use the brush until you have done this. For outlining axles, uprights, or any parts with straight lines, use the pen and a straight edge, and for curved parts use an architectural curve instead of the straight edge. Architectural curves may be bought for a few cents at any artists'

—

material shop. After you have gone over all the outlines with the ruling pen, it is quite easy to work up to the lines with a brush.

It is important to remember at every stage that nothing but the best work will satisfy an engineer. His whole education and professional training have made him accurate and exacting in a high degree. And he expects as much scrupulous care from others. You must be prepared to find these good qualities sometimes carried to an extreme. The writer remembers once submitting a mounted 14 x 17 photograph to a manager of a large engineering firm. This man had the instinct for precision so strongly developed that, as soon as he took the photograph in his hands, he said, *"It is not mounted square."* Sure enough, when the rule was applied, it was found that there was one-sixty-fourth of an inch more white margin showing on one side than on the other—a fault that would never have been noticed by any ordinary man. Here was a man, however, who had been trained throughout a long life to working to a thousandth part of an inch. And the want of exactness in the mounting worried him so much that he could hardly bring himself to consider the photograph at all.

That was an extreme instance, of course. Speaking broadly, engineers are seldom unreasonable. You will generally find them ready to help you in every way possible. Their technical and practical experience makes them more ready than other commercial men to appreciate the difficulties under which you may be working. If the conditions are so unfavorable as to make it impossible for you to take a satisfactory photograph of a piece of machinery, it is always wise to explain the position frankly to the engineer in charge—and his practical mind will almost invariably hit upon some way out of your difficulty.

If there is not room in your town for two photographers, all you have to do is to secure the greater portion of the work, and the other man will clear out.

RETOUCHING HINTS.

Negatives which have to be retouched should be carefully rubbed with cotton when taken from the washing water. If they are simply rinsed, and put in the rack to dry, there is almost certain to be a deposit of lime or other substance left on their surfaces. This deposit is a cause of trouble when the negatives pass into the retouchers' hands. Unless the medium is rubbed all over the negatives there will be transparent patches where the medium has rubbed off some of the deposit. These patches will show in the prints. Furthermore, some of the deposit will have become so firmly attached to the film that the medium will not have removed it. This will cause a grittiness which is very annoying to the retoucher.

If the retoucher finds that the deposit has been left on a negative, he should clean the surface with alcohol and a soft rag before applying the medium.

Unless a negative is absolutely dry the pencil will dig into the film, and the work will be scratchy. It is always a good plan to warm the negative in front of a fire, or over a gas ring, before starting retouching. This will get rid of any moisture absorbed from the atmosphere. The negative must be allowed to cool before applying the medium.

Greasiness of the film is a frequent source of annoyance to the retoucher. When this is met with, the negative should be immersed in a 2 per cent. solution of ammonia for a minute, rubbed gently with a piece of cotton, washed for a quarter of an hour and then dried.

It is a mistake to use one kind of medium for all classes of work. A fairly thick or "tacky" medium should be used for large negatives with masses of shadow which have to be filled up broadly. A much thinner medium is necessary when working on small negatives with fine detail. The "tacky" medium takes the pencil freely. This is an advantage in large negatives where a certain amount of roughness is not a drawback. The thin medium takes up less lead, thus helping to keep the work close and fine which is always desirable in small pictures with fine detail.

When you have put all the lead you can on a part of a negative, and you want to add just a little more, it is a good plan to fold up a tube of paper and to breathe slowly through it on to the part of the film requiring more work. This will revive the tooth of the medium, and restore its stickiness, when a little more work can be added. The negative must be well dried after this treatment before printing.

It is not generally known that a negative may be given a matte surface, without injuring the film, by rubbing all over it with fine pumice powder. Only the finest pumice should be used for this purpose, and the best way to apply it is to rub it on with the palm of the hand working with a circular motion. Any amount of work can be done on a film treated in this way. It is a useful method for improving large negatives containing harsh contrasts, but it is not recommended for small pictures with delicate detail.

So many new methods for toning down harsh lights have sprung up in recent years, that some of the older ones have been almost forgotten. Some retouchers with long years of experience, however, say that they have found nothing better than ordinary ink eraser for rubbing down very dense patches in a negative. The best way to use it is to take a piece of thin celluloid and in it cut an opening the size of the patch to be rubbed down. When this is laid on the negative the ink eraser can be used freely without the risk of damaging the surrounding parts. It is wise to practice before using this method on regular work.

The study of anatomy is almost essential to the retoucher who wants to produce really good work. It is not necessary that he should know the names of all the facial muscles; his studies should be directed more to the careful observation of living faces than to learning long strings of Latin names from text books. A great deal can be learned by looking at engraved or etched portraits by good artists. The direction of the lines should be carefully studied. It will be seen that, as a rule, the lines follow the contour of the various forms of the features. For instance, the lines of shading of the nose, mouth, eyelids and ear generally follow the forms of the particular parts they represent.

The forehead is generally over-retouched by inexperienced workers. One look at a forehead will show that it is not a flat surface, but that it is made up of a series of undulating curves. It should not, therefore, be worked up until it is of one even tint all over. There is an old saying among painters that the highest light in a portrait should be the part that would first get wet in a shower of rain falling in the same direction as the light is falling upon the sitter. In ordinary studio lighting this would be the forehead. As a rule, then, this is where the highest light, apart from the reflection in the eye, should be in a photograph.

In working up hair it should be remembered that the touch required is quite a short line. It is hair in the mass, and not a number of separate hairs that should be represented by the retouching. You cannot work in such a way that each pencil line represents one hair. If you attempt this you will make the hair in the portrait look like wire or string.

Everyone knows that when the corners of the mouth turn down they give a sad expression to the face, and that when they turn up the expression is suggestive of mirth. The matter, however, is not quite so simple as this statement would suggest. Every expression is not a question of one feature only but of the whole face. In laughter the upturned corners of the mouth alter the lines between the nose and the mouth. At the same time the cheeks are raised and little lines appear 'round the corners of the eyes. These points should be remembered when altering the expression of a portrait.

The wrinkles which gather at the outer corners of the eyes must not always be regarded as a sign of age. They are often found in young people of a happy disposition. In fact, these lines come and go in most people as the cheeks are raised in laughter or lowered when the features are in repose. It is quite a mistake then, for the retoucher to make a

FROM AN ARTURA IRIS PRINT, BY MORRISON STUDIO.

point of always working out "crow's feet" in all portraits except those of old people.

———

Excerpts from the Diary of

April 2. I've just been looking at the new portrait albums and there's one thing about them that I don't like. They're handsome, practical and thoroughly worth while in every way but their present location is all wrong. A salesman that spent all his time in the home office wouldn't be worth much to the company that employed him. That's the way with these portrait albums. As long as they stay in the studio they're loafing. They ought to be out selling photographs. The immediate profit doesn't interest me so much as does the fact that every album we sell is going to declare periodical dividends in the years to come. They're the best advertising medium that a studio ever had. They're a constant invitation to "make that appointment to-day". They're a steady reminder of the pleasure that portraits can provide. Consequently we're going to push albums.

The old gentleman and I are looking at this portrait album proposition from the same angle. He believes that we should feature it in our newspaper advertising and that a personal letter to a selected list of studio patrons would be good business. It's funny to hear him talk like this when a couple of years ago he used to rest his head on a soft focus lens, open his mouth to stop 4 and sleep all day.

April 8. "In the spring the young man's fancy neck-wear lightly turns——" etc. The poet said something like that once and he had love located at just about the right latitude and longitude. I've got a funny feeling myself this time of year but believe me Willie Twinkle, the soda water clerk, has got it in its most acute stage—you can tell it by his necktie. The tie has that subdued tint so characteristic of a fire in a blast furnace. It looks as if it had been re-developed in a rainbow.

The girl in the case is Mildred Simple and as she and her mother are staying at the Mansion House I have plenty of opportunity of seeing Willie and Mildred groping through love's young dream. Willie is received in the hotel parlor after his spectrum tie has announced his presence, by Mildred and her mother. The parlor is very gloomy and very big and Willie after he has tripped over a chair or two and stepped on Mrs. Simple's feet to show that he feels perfectly at ease, selects with unerring instinct the chair furthest from the one Mildred occupies and sits down. Mildred can just make him out across the yard after yard of faded pink carpet. When he talks she sees his lips move before the sound of his voice reaches her. Mrs. Simple is having a lovely time. She watches the young people like a cat and nips in the bud all attempts at light heartedness. Mildred tries to make the best of the situation. She laughs at everything Willie says and at everything her mother says and the rest of the time vainly tries to think of something to say, herself. Willie seems unaware of the fact that the seat of his chair would probably fit the view and is perched on the extreme edge as if ready to jump into space any instant. He swallows a great deal for no apparent reason and whenever he does his Adam's apple strikes his high stiff collar with a brisk click. About ten o'clock he says that he must be going and that he has had a very nice time and Mildred says "Wasn't it fun?"

One of these days the old lady is going to drop in at the drug store for a soda and Willie is going to give her a nice little glass of prussic acid.

* * *

When photographing a street, view, take no notice of the crowd of children who want to be in the picture, until you have focused and put the plate in position. Then go 'round to the front of the camera, pull the focusing cloth over your head, and pretend to be taking the view in the opposite direction to the one you have focused. In a few minutes the children will move to the back of the camera, and you can quickly expose your plate.

Net weight as in illustration 10 lbs.

The Ley Collapsible Skylight

Improved Model C.

The first and original square collapsible skylight to fold like an umbrella. Beware of imitations. Pat. Sept. 22, 1916

IT IS A FLASH LAMP THAT NEVER FAILS

The hood can be raised to a height of eleven feet, if required.

The screen is 36 x 42. It is properly fireproofed, transparent and smoke proof.

The Improved Lighting Ignition System assures the Photographer that the lamp will go every time.

Price with case, - - - - - - $30.00

SWEET, WALLACH & COMPANY
EASTMAN KODAK COMPANY
CHICAGO, ILL.

NEW BACKGROUNDS. Ask for New 1917 Background Booklet. Cut 1682.

No. 1682—A New Background specially designed for group work, nothing ever painted at the price.

Prices painted in **Black and White or Sepia**

8 x 10	$16.00
9 x 12	21.60
10 x 15	30.00

The scenic part of the ground may be painted in oil colors at an extra charge of 10 cents per square foot.

For Sale By SWEET, WALLACH & COMPANY, Eastman Kodak Company, CHICAGO

Graduation Days

This is the season when warm days usher in the dainty frocks of graduation and the fresh, informal garb of holiday time.

Parents realize that the passing of school days marks an important epoch in the lives of their children and so desire to perpetuate, through appropriate photographs, the memories of this period.

Progressive photographers appreciate these opportunities for profitable business and are prepared with appropriate offerings.

The Collins Line is rich in suitable folders for school work. We suggest, in particular, Alda, Blenheim and Campus—the A B C of school mountings, made in appropriate sizes and colors.

For illustrations and descriptions of these folders, see our new general Catalog or, better still, send coin or stamps for samples **Four** cents for Blenheim and **Two** cents for Alda or Campus.

"Collins Mountings Mark the Channel to Better Prices"

A. M. Collins Mfg. Company
PHILADELPHIA   PENNSYLVANIA

SIMPLEX AUTO PRINT DRYER

A Dryer for the Large Studio, the Commercial Photographer or the Amateur Finisher who must dry prints quickly.

Perfectly dried prints, either single or double weight, in less than 4 minutes.

Price, $150.00

For further information write

Sweet, Wallach & Company Inc

EASTMAN KODAK COMPANY
CHICAGO

WE REALIZE

That Service is a factor of first importance to the Photographer.

In choosing our stock we have been guided by that thought, and by the results of years of experience.

We aim to carry in stock Everything for the Photographer.

When your order comes in we can usually *ship complete* the same day it is received.

Chicago is fortunately situated, its Railroad Service being the best in the world.

Send your orders to

SWEET, WALLACH & COMPANY
EASTMAN KODAK COMPANY
CHICAGO, ILL.

Century Studio Outfit

A NECESSITY
For the up-to-date Studio

THE No. 7 Studio Outfit embodies the highest degree of efficiency with richness of finish and design.

The Camera is made of selected mahogany and cherry, highly polished; the metal parts are lacquered brass. It is fitted with a Sliding Carriage and Spring-Actuating Reversible Ground Glass Frame and Eastman View Camera Plate or Cut Film Holders, permitting exposures on full plate in either horizontal or vertical positions. By using diaphragms furnished, two exposures can be made on the 8 x 10 plate. There is also furnished a 5 x 7 Adapter Back for 5 x 7 plates, vertical or horizontal.

The stand is the regular No. 1 Semi-Centennial, which has proven to be the most popular on the market.

The Price

Century Studio Outfit No. 7 Complete, consists of the 8 x 10 Camera with sliding Ground Glass Carriage, including one 8 x 10 and one 5 x 7 Adapter Back, with 8 x 10 and 5 x 7 Eastman View Plate or Cut Film Holder and Semi-Centennial Stand. **Price, $104.00.**

Complete List of Century Outfits.

Number 7 Century Studio Outfit, 8 x 10, complete, ...	$104.00
Number 8 Century Studio Outfit, 11 x 14, complete, ...	156.00
Number 2 Century Grand Outfit, 8 x 10, complete, ...	129.00
Number 2 Century Grand Outfit, 11 x 14, complete, ...	164.00
Number 4 Century Studio Outfit, 8 x 10, complete, ...	69.00
Number 5 Century Studio Outfit, 5 x 7, complete, ...	76.00
Universal Century Studio Outfit, 8 x 10, complete, ...	117.00
Universal Century Studio Outfit, 11 x 14, complete, ...	154.00

Write for prices on Outfits or parts thereof with Lenses and Shutters.

FOR PROMPT AND SATISFACTORY SERVICE SEND YOUR ORDERS TO

SWEET, WALLACH & COMPANY

Eastman Kodak Company
133 North Wabash Ave., CHICAGO

THE LARGEST PHOTO SUPPLY HOUSE IN THE WORLD.

All outfits illustrated in No. 39, Sweet, Wallach & Company Catalog.

Add an Air Brush to Your Equipment

Any photographer can easily learn to use it. It will improve your work and pay for itself many times over in the course of a year.

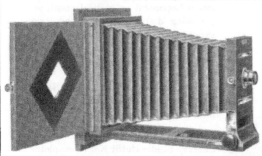

We illustrate the new model A1 Wold Air Brush—exact size.

These brushes we carry in stock and recommend to the photographer who wants to add to the selling value of his photographs. Price, $22.00.

You will be surprised at the number of things you **can do with an Air Brush.**

For Beginners— **"A TREATISE ON THE AIR BRUSH"** by Frazer, price $1.50, will be a great help. It is a clothbound book, the contents of which embody a series of illustrated lessons.

For Sale by SWEET, WALLACH & CO., (Eastman Kodak Co.,) CHICAGO, ILL.

REVOLVING BACK ENLARGING CAMERA

The Revolving Back Enlarging Camera is simple, efficient and practical, incorporating all necessary adjustments for making Enlargements easily and accurately.

The Negative Carrier is fitted with Nested Spring Kits, taking all standard size negatives from 8 x 10 down to 3¼ x 4¼. The Spring Fingers are attached to the kits with split rivets.

Focusing is done with rack and pinion.

Any suitable light may be used with the Revolving Back Enlarging Camera, with Condensers or without.

THE PRICE

Revolving Back Enlarging Camera Complete with 8 x 10 Revolving Negative Carrier, with Spring Finger Kits and a sheet of Opal Glass 11½ x 11½ Without lens, - - - $35.00

SWEET, WALLACH & COMPANY (Eastman Kodak Company) CHICAGO. Ill

---

IMPROVED MODEL EASTMAN ENLARGING OUTFIT

Makes every kind of Enlargement and Lantern Slides as well. You need it every day.

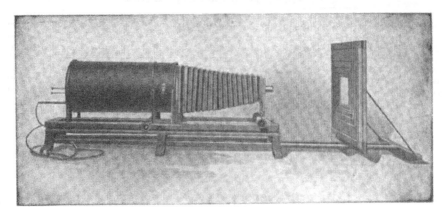

PRICE—Eastman Enlarging Outfit, including 500 watt Nitrogen Mazda Lamp, without lens - - $100.00
Nitrogen Mazda Lamp, 500 watt, Concentrated Filament, - - - - - - - 7.50
Carrier, not including Nitrogen Mazda Lamp, - - - - - - - - - 7.50

SWEET, WALLACH & COMPANY (Eastman Kodak Company) CHICAGO, ILL.

The KRONER PHOTO PRINT DRYER
is a Necessity

where a large number of prints must be dried in a limited time.

No long tables or numerous blotters required.   The feeding and releasing is continuous.   **The belt will not wrinkle nor will it harm the finest print,** and same is of sufficient weight to keep the prints from the extreme heat.

The important points of construction :

1—All adjustments are cast from patterns
2—The worm gear is enclosed in a dust proof housing
3—The drum heads are made of sheet steel
4—Every roller is re-enforced with a casting at ends
5—The machine is mounted on casters and can be easily moved.

Large machine. Price **$175.00** net F. O. B. St. Louis
Small   "   "   **$135.00** "   "   "   "   "   "

Copyright E. A. KRONER 1916

THE KRONER PHOTO PRINT DRYER CO.
St. Louis, Mo.   Clayton Branch.

Something Easy to Sell

Every Salesman—no matter what his line—is delighted to get his hands on Something New, because he knows it will be Easy to Sell.

Mr. Photographer!   You are a Salesman, and you want Something New and Easy to Sell.

You don't want your show case one deadly monotony of style and Color.   Introduce Variety—make your work Seasonable—Keep it alive. Last season's styles are as dead as a last year's newspaper.   Throw them out.   Get the New Goods in sight.

We have in stock about 40 of the New 1917 Styles of Mountings. Our salesmen will be pleased to show them.

A Complete Sample Set of Taprell, Loomis & Company's 22 New Styles sent prepaid for 75 cents, the 75 cents being refunded on an order for $5.00 worth of the New Goods.

SWEET, WALLACH & COMPANY
EASTMAN KODAK COMPANY
CHICAGO, ILL.

The Selling Habit.

Sometimes a man spends ten dollars' worth of time trying to save, and in the end saves only a dime. Get out of that habit if you have it. The saving habit may have some advantages but it certainly can be overdone. Your time and mental energy should be spent where it brings the biggest returns.

The *Photograph Business* is a *Selling Business*—Your whole energy should be directed toward the sales—the materials will scarcely cost 20% of the selling price of the pictures. Suppose, by close buying or saving, you could reduce this cost 10%; that would be only 2% of the total selling price of the pictures—A sale is always 100% real money, therefore the time spent in Selling is 50 times more valuable than the time spent in Saving.

Keep saying it over to yourself "This is a Selling Business—Selling is what brings the money"—After you have convinced yourself you will not be fussing about trifling changes in the cost of materials, and your Sales will show that you have something really worth selling.

Get the Selling Habit.

You Don't Have To Talk Them—

The Public Asks For Cirkut Pictures—

There are opportunities in every locality—One job often pays for the Outfit.

CIRKUTS are made in 5 sizes for film 5, 6½, 8, 10, 12 and 16 inches in width—

Price No. 5 Outfit Complete - - - - - - - -	$118.00
Price No. 6 Outfit Complete - - - - - - - -	126.50
Price No. 8 Outfit Complete - - - - - - - -	190.00
Price No. 10 Outfit Complete - - - - - - - -	300.00
Price No. 16 Outfit Complete - - - - - - - -	445.00

If interested, ask for illustrated booklet " The Cirkut Method " giving details of Outfit and prices on various lens equipments.

SWEET, WALLACH & CO., Eastman Kodak Co., CHICAGO, ILL.

REMBRANDT.

Why did the name of Rembrandt get mixed up with photographic portraiture? Advertisements and circulars sent out by professionals often contain such terms as: "Rembrandt Studies," "Rembrandt Lightings," "Rembrandt Portraits," or "Rembrandt Heads." Apart from the name, there is usually nothing about these portraits to suggest the influence of this famous painter. It was the custom a few years ago to apply the name "Rembrandt" to any portrait with strong contrasts of light and shade. Why? Nobody can say.

A striking, and sometimes very pleasing portrait may be made by taking a sitter in profile, with the features sharply defined by a line of light against a dark background. But there is no reason whatever for naming this kind of work after Rembrandt. In fact, nothing could be further removed from Rembrandt's art than portraits of this class. At the same time, it must not be inferred that Rembrandt's influence is not apparent in much good work turned out by our leading professionals. There are some who have profited greatly by the study of his paintings. They do not imitate his wonderful portraits, they do better than that. They learn the lessons that his work teaches. But the strange thing is, that the only photographs that show any relationship to Rembrandt are never named after him, while those without the faintest family likeness bear his name.

There is not much left for a man to learn, in the art of composition and the management of light and shade, if he has extracted all the knowledge that has been worked into one of Rembrandt's portraits. Compare a so-called photographic "Rembrandt" with a good copy of one of the artist's masterpieces. Take each picture as it appeals to the eye at a first look. To most people the photograph will appear more striking. This is important. Good art is seldom ostentatious, it is never startling, it is never catchy, it does not shout. It is quiet, calm and simple. Its beauty steals into our minds. It wins our admiration, and does not demand attention by a display of fireworks. The effect produced by a striking pic-

ture passes away as quickly as it comes. A good work of art grows upon us. We like it more and more as time goes on. We are able to live with it. When Sir Joshua Reynolds visited the picture galleries at Rome he had to ask to be shown the Raphaels. Before he left Italy they were the only pictures he could see.

Notice the way Rembrandt massed his lights and shades. Spottiness is fatal to breadth and harmony. If lights and shades are scattered all over a picture, an irritating patchwork effect is produced, the eye finds no resting-place, and the mind is put into a state of confusion.

Rembrandt loved large masses of shadow and half-tone. He painted in a very low key. In fact, fully two-thirds of all the canvas that he covered represents shadow. But in all the shadow there is detail. It is felt by the beholder rather than actually shown by the artist. In looking at the lowest-toned Rembrandt, the feeling is produced that the eye can penetrate into the remotest corners and deepest recesses, although very little detail is really painted. His shadows are shadows, not solid walls of blackness. A good picture suggests more than it reveals. It is just here that so many photographers fail when attempting work in a low key. Their shadows have not that luminous or transparent quality; they give no suggestion of air and space behind the sitter, and they do not produce the feeling that there is nothing more in the picture than the eye actually sees.

Whether we work in a low key or a high one, the most important point of all is correct tonal values. Rembrandt never went very high up in the scale of tones; he pitched his highest note, and from that he worked step by step down into his deepest shadow. Again compare your photograph with the copy of the painting. In the photograph there is a series of jumps from the highest light to the deepest shadow, while in the painting the scale is descended by an almost infinite number of short easy steps. Some photographers think that they can compensate for the lack of tone by fuzziness. Softness in a photograph is not produced in this way. It can be brought about only by correct rendering of tones. Rembrandt produced his effects by straight and honest work, and his pictures are real object lessons to both painters and photographers.

We are in the midst of our Easter business, and it is coming up to expectations, but we are not letting any chances for new business slip by. I mention this because the average busy photographer would not have jumped at a bit of speculative work—possibly I had better call it advertising—when the studio was already working right up to capacity on Easter orders.

What the receptionist advises seems to go, however, and I guess it will until I show poor judgment, and this is not to be the case if I can help it. I feel that my bread and butter depends upon the judgment I use— and I do a lot of thinking to keep my head work properly balanced.

We have a cavalry troop of which we are very proud—and with good reason. It is made up of boys from the best families in town and every one of them can be counted on to do his bit if his country needs him.

These boys have been down on the border for almost a year, but the welcome report that they had been ordered home finally came. Of course, there was lots of excitement and a great many mothers and fathers were made happy.

Elaborate preparations were made for their reception and the course of their journey was closely followed. I happened to meet one boy's father on the car the other day and he told me the troop would probably reach M— on Monday morning and would stop there to take their horses from the train and exercise them, when they would again entrain and reach home in the evening.

As soon as we reached Main Street, I rushed into the up-town ticket office for a time table and by the time I reached the studio, my plans were made.

The troop train was traveling slowly, and if one of our men with the Graflex could go to M— and get the pictures I wanted in an hour after the troop arrived, he would have several chances of getting home three or four hours ahead of the troop's arrival in our town.

We tried it out and my luck was with me. Our man was back at twelve-twenty, and at three o'clock we had enlargements from some of the negatives in our display case. As soon as the second lot was finished we put the new display in our case and the first display in the bank window, the bank having closed by this time.

It reminded me of newspaper "scoops" I have read about—and it *was* a scoop. The train was delayed and didn't get in until after dark, so aside from a rather poor flashlight, our pictures of the home-coming were the only ones that really counted. They proved a good second day drawing card and the Boss was more than pleased with the advertising.

We didn't sell any of the pictures to the boys, as they were more in the nature of news pictures. We gave the enlargements to the troop and were satisfied with the advertising we received from them. Every man in the troop saw our display case, and every one of them knows we are live photographers, so we will surely get some of their business— in fact, we have already had some business from them.

The Boss and I considered offering a free sitting to each of the boys with the idea of making up an album and presenting it to the troop with our compliments, but we decided this smacked too much of speculative methods. I am glad we didn't, for I have been able to put the same idea across without the bad feature.

I had another talk with the boy's father who gave me my first idea, and I worked around the subject in such a way that he got the album idea himself. He called me up to-day and asked me to see him—and you can be sure I did.

We are going to photograph each member of the troop and have a special album made to hold the pictures, and the boys' fathers are going to present the finished album to the Captain.

We are doing our part of the work at a reasonable price and will be paid for our time and material, and you can rest assured that I will get some good orders out of this lot of sittings.

I am glad our enthusiasm didn't run away with our good judgment, for we have never made free sittings in this studio since I have been its receptionist.

CAUSES OF WEAK NEGATIVES.

Professionals sometimes get a batch of weak negatives, and very often are unable to discover the reason. It may arise from any one of three causes. Two of them—under-exposure on account of poor light and under-development on account of the developer being too cold are likely to be encountered during the winter months. The third cause is one which is to be found summer and winter alike. It is the use of a developer containing chemicals which are below the proper strength.

If a formula has the proper proportions of pyro, sulphite and carbonate, either by weight or hydrometer test, and it gives weak negatives, do not try to get more density by increasing the amount of pyro. The probability is that the developer is lacking in carbonate.

As every professional knows, the function of carbonate in the developer is to act as an accelerator. It opens the pores of the gelatine and helps the reducing agent, pyro, to act more freely on the granules of silver which have been exposed to the light.

The plate-maker gives you a developer formula which assumes that carbonate of a certain strength will be used. Directly you use a carbonate which does not come up to this standard you alter the working of the developer. It is necessary to take into consideration the difference between the various brands of carbonate of soda. Two brands of carbonate might test the same when dissolved in water, but one would have a stronger alkaline reaction than the other. Many brands contain large quantities of bi-carbonate which, though helping to raise the hydrometer test, do not have an accelerating action in the developer. The hydrometer only shows the amount of solids in solution—the test has no value unless the nature of the solids is known. For this reason E. K. Co. Tested Carbonate of Soda, which must contain more than a certain high percentage of pure carbonate before it can pass the laboratory test, would not weigh more, or test higher, than an equal quantity of carbonate containing impurities. The difference in the developing action, however, would be unmistakably shown in the negative.

There is probably no chemical which varies so much in strength in different brands of carbonate of soda. E. K. Co. Tested Carbonate is uniform in strength and action, and its increasing popularity among professionals is undoubtedly due to this fact. By using Tested Carbonate you remove the chief cause of weak, flat negatives.

In nearly every photographic process the strength and purity of the chemicals used are of as much importance as the strength of the carbonate in the developer. You can easily safeguard yourself by always using E. K. Co. Tested Chemicals. They have to stand the most searching analytical tests in the Kodak laboratories because it is of vital importance to the Eastman Kodak Co. that their plates and papers should be worked to the best advantage by their customers. It was to remove one of the chief causes of inferior work that E. K. Co. Tested Chemicals were placed on the market. The sign of that guarantee is the E. K. Co. Tested Chemical Seal.

OUTDOOR GROUPS.

Although its profit-making possibilities are well known, this branch of photography, from an artistic point of view, lags a long way behind the regular professional portraiture. There is certainly plenty of room for improvement in the pictorial quality of group work.

But there are difficulties in group photography that the man who only does ordinary studio portraiture knows nothing about. It is well worth a little trouble and patience to become an expert, because there is a big demand for groups.

In arranging a group, the first principle to consider is simplicity. This means avoiding awkward lines, abrupt angles, overcrowded parts and distracting meaningless accessories.

The next point to consider is unity. If a group is to have any pictorial value at all, there must be a theme that connects the component parts. This theme should be emphasized by the arrangement of the figures, or by the concentration of interest. For instance, in football or baseball groups, the captain can be doing something—describing a point in the game, for example—in which all the members are obviously interested. In a family group, the mother can be explaining a toy to a child. It is seldom wise to place the chief figure of a group in the center of the picture. The effect is much more pleasing, and the emphasis is far stronger, if a point somewhere between the center and the edge of the picture is chosen. When the line of heads rises towards the middle, the pictorial effect is much better than when it curves down. The heads should never be placed at equal distances from one another.

The placing of light and dark dresses is a point of great importance in group making. It sems to be the desire of some operators to produce a chess-board pattern in their pictures. They do this by arranging the figures in such a way that light and dark dresses alternate throughout the group. The effect is always spotty and irritating.

The lights and shades should not be scattered; they should be collected and arranged in masses. It is a good plan to put the figures in light clothes together near the center and arrange the other figures so that they form a border round the mass of light. Very rarely indeed should those wearing dark clothes be placed in the middle of the group, and those wearing light at the edges.

With regard to backgrounds, the operator generally has to make the best of what is provided for him. But where a choice can be made, appropriate surroundings, with as little obtrusive detail as possible, should be selected. For example, a house party at some country home should be shown with part of the building as a background, rather than with an unimportant corner of the garden, where flowers and shrubs obtrude and cause distracting white spots.

Above everything else, do not allow the sitters to stare at the camera. Nothing helps so much to give a frozen, stiff and lifeless appearance to a group, as this cold, blank staring of every pair of eyes in the picture.

Self-consciousness is often difficult to deal with in an individual portrait, but when a number of persons get together for a group, the difficulty is increased out of all proportion to their number. Everybody wants to look his or her best, but dare not make any visible effort to do so, lest it calls forth a volume of good-natured chaff from the other members of the group. This is where the personal influence of the operator is most valuable. He must go about his work cheerfully, and with a joke here, a serious word there, quickly, but without blustering, get his group composed. Of course, there is the "funny man" to contend with—the man, generally a young one, who will persist in trying to make the others giggle just when the exposure is going to be made. This man needs careful handling. Polite severity, plain speaking, and a dignified manner, combined with patience, will generally make him keep quiet.

There is more money left in group photography than has ever been taken out of it—but the man who makes himself an expert is the only one who will get hold of it.

This album takes 87 per cent. of the sizes of portraits now made by photographers.

Eastman Portrait Albums

Will stimulate business by inviting portraits and offering a practical and dignified means of preserving them. The three styles of leaves furnished in each album have openings, back of which are mats suitable for several smaller sized prints. This ingenious arrangement adapts the album to a wide variety of styles and sizes of prints and overcomes the only obstacle to reviving the usefulness and popularity of the home portrait album.

The albums are bound in black, long grained leather with the word "Portraits" stamped in gold leaf on the cover. Leaves are furnished for 2, 4, 6 and 8 prints and the album may be enlarged, by means of extra leaves, to twice its normal capacity.

LIST PRICE.

Eastman Portrait Album, either vertical or horizontal, including 12 assorted leaves, ... $10.00
Extra leaves for any size opening, each .40

EASTMAN KODAK COMPANY,
ROCHESTER, N. Y.

At your dealer's.

WANTED

DISCARDED NEGATIVES

We purchase Discarded Negatives of standard size from $4\frac{1}{4}$ x $6\frac{1}{2}$ to 14 x 17, in shipments weighing 100 lbs. or more, providing same are in good condition and packed carefully, in accordance with our instructions.

Before making any shipment please secure these instructions, prices and further particulars which will be furnished on application.

EASTMAN KODAK COMPANY,
ROCHESTER, N. Y.

Department S.

EASTMAN FILM
DEVELOPING HOLDER No. 2

This is an improved, horizontal shape holder that may be used in the same tanks used for Core Plate Developing Racks. The top bar rests on the edges of tank, four clips securely hold the film in place and a hook permits the holder to be suspended while film is drying.

THE PRICE.

5 x 7, ...	$0.30
8 x 10, ...	.50
Eastman Film Loading Fixture:	
5 x 7, ...	1.25
8 x 10, ...	1.50

CORE PLATE
DEVELOPING RACKS

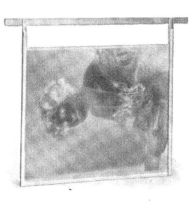

For holding plates during developing, fixing, washing and drying. They permit the plates to be handled conveniently with little danger of scratches or finger marks. The racks are made of metal that will not corrode and may be used in any tank of proper dimensions.

THE PRICE EACH

4¼ x 6½, . .	$ .50	8 x 10, . .	$ .60
5 x 7, . .	.50	10 x 12, . .	1.10
6½ x 8½, . .	.60	11 x 14, .	1.60

EASTMAN KODAK COMPANY,
ROCHESTER, N. Y.

All dealers'.

Century Studio Outfits

WHEN you place your customer before a Century Studio Outfit, he instinctively feels a sense of confidence in you and your work that will help when the proofs are shown.

Obsolete apparatus in your light room produces the opposite effect.

A new Century Studio Outfit will help to better sales.

Send for Professional Catalog.

Century Camera Division
Eastman Kodak Co.,
ROCHESTER, N. Y.

Lightning Source UK Ltd.
Milton Keynes UK
UKOW06f2022300913

218239UK00007B/150/P

Railways & Recollections 1961

BLAENGWYNFI

Series Introduction

Railway publishing has been around almost as long as the railways themselves and there have been countless books with a historical theme, telling the story of a particular line, say, and occasionally linking the subject to its social context, but never before has there been, in such an accessible way, a juxtapositioning of photographic illustration of a railway subject with the events, happenings and highlights of a wider sphere and calendar. This series will, initially, take a particular year and place the views displayed alongside a carefully selected pot-pourri of what happened in that twelve-month period. The vast majority of the images in the first few books are from the Ray Ruffell collection, held by the publisher, but material from other sources will be interspersed where felt necessary to maintain appropriate variety. Ray was a railwayman and photographer of equal merit and the main criterion for inclusion in these books is for the images to be both interesting and aesthetically pleasing within a chosen theme.

The books are aimed at a more general market than mere railway aficionados or enthusiasts and the authors hope and trust that they will be sure in their aim and that you, the reader, will find much to enjoy, appreciate, enthuse about and even smile about! And it is hoped that some of your own memories are stirred along the way and that you may wish to share these with friends!

© Peter Townsend and John Stretton 2008
Photos: © The NOSTALGIA Collection archive unless otherwise credited.

Contents

First published in 2008
ISBN 978 1 85794 292 7
Silver Link Publishing Ltd
The Trundle
Ringstead Road
Great Addington
Kettering
Northants NN14 4BW

Tel/Fax: 01536 330588
email: sales@nostalgiacollection.com
Website: www.nostalgiacollection.com
British Library Cataloguing in Publication Data
A catalogue record for this book is available from the British Library.
Printed and bound in Great Britain

Frontispiece: **BLAENGWYNFI** We are just in 1961, on 30 December and snow lies on and around the station but the fireman is still in short sleeves, despite the cold. Exacerbated by the cold, steam wraps itself around the coaches of the 2.33 p.m. to Bridgend. On the Rhondda & Swansea Bay Line from Port Talbot to Treherbert, we are here looking towards the 3,443 yd long Rhondda Tunnel, dug beneath the hillside seen in the distance, but the train will be travelling in the opposite direction. Ex-GWR 0-6-0PT 9660 was a relatively new engine, emerging from, Swindon Works in December 1946 and spending its entire life working in South Wales – apart from a brief six month spell at Bristol (Barrow Road) shed. The end came, from Neath shed, on 22 November 1964

Opposite background: **MERTHYR** Looking back towards Merthyr from the Dowlais (Caer Harris) to Ystrad Mynach train on 7 October 1961. The train was made up of 2 carriages behind 0-6-2T No 5610 from which the smoke drifts back across the valley.

Introduction

This is the 9th volume in the series and for regular readers/collectors the concept should be familiar. We have been pleased with the overall reaction to the first few volumes which has been generally favourable. The old saying goes that you cannot please all the people all of the time and of course this is as true of this series and the individual volume content as it is with anything else in life! Hopefully as the series grows, and we trust that, with sufficient support from our readers, it will, imbalances between say regions or locomotive types, steam or diesel, goods or passenger etc will become increasingly balanced when taken as a whole. We do of course welcome constructive feedback and will endeavour to bear this in mind when making selections for future volumes.

Although predominantly railway based the series will from time to time include Recollections based on other forms of transport, but again the pictures will all be from the year under review. *Blackpool Trams & Recollections 1973* by *Barry Macoughlin* was the first such volume and *Midland Red 1959* by David Harvey has just joined the fold as we write this.

So to this volume...

As 1961 dawned it would no longer be possible to spend a Farthing! The last minted examples were issued in 1956, the first, in silver, having been issued in 1279! The Morris Minor had by now become a motoring legend and the 1 millionth example rolled off the production lines. The Common Market was even then making headlines as Britain applied for membership and Iraq was in the news as Britain sent troops to Kuwait in July as an invasion by Iraq seemed imminent. They were withdrawn by the end of September as no attack materialised. The A6 murder took place in August resulting in the hanging of James Hanratty in April 1962, the case became the subject of one of the longest appeals in British legal history. Adolf Eichman was found guilty in December at the Nuremberg War Crimes trials and sentenced to hang.

On the railways Dr Richard Beeching was appointed to head up British Railways - a decision that was to have considerable influence on the future of the network. The East Coast main line for so long the domain of the A3 and A4s on express passenger services began to see the start of the Diesel take over. *The Flying Scotsman* and *Talisman* named expresses for example became predominantly Deltic hauled in the summer and the gradual decline in steam dominance had begun. Line closures during the year were in fact quite modest with a total of around 150 route miles being lost. The Glasgow Suburban Electrification known as *The Blue Trains* - the first stage of which had opened the previous year- 're-opened' to traffic in November following the rectification of serious problems with transformers that had led to the withdrawal of electric trains for some 11 months. The last passenger steam train ran on the London Underground, although steam haulage of maintenance trains lasted a further another 10 years.

Elsewhere *Mothercare* opened their first shop in Kingston-on-Thames, new Universities were announced for Coventry, Colchester and Canterbury, all of which are of course now firmly established. The Space Race hotted up with the USSR winning the first man in space prize as Uri Gagarin left the earth's atmosphere and entered the history books. The USA were close on their heels putting Alan Shepard into space just under two weeks later.

In the world of Pop Music the swinging sixties were rocking and smooching to such sounds as *Poetry in Motion* from Johnny Tilotson, *Runaway* from Del Shannon and *You don't know* and *Walkin' back to happiness* both from Helen Shapiro. Cliff Richards, Elvis Presley, The Everly Brothers and Petula Clark were amongst many favourite artists to enjoy No 1 hits during the year and in this year, Duane Eddy was voted NME's top World Personality, ahead of Elvis to whom he had been runne-up in 1960 and 1962.. This then is Railways & Recollections for 1961 enjoy...

Peter Townsend   *John Stretton*
Northamptonshire   *Oxfordshire*
              February 2008

Above: **ABERBEEG** Fx-GWR 0-6-0PT 4627 trundles through Aberbeeg station platforms with a mixed freight on 22 September, its exhaust betraying the hard work up the grade towards Brynmawr, via the Western Valleys Line. New from Swindon in September 1946, early work was from Gloucester, with its move to Aberbeeg coming in January 1959. The engine shed at Aberbeeg closed as a fully functioning depot on 1 January 1961, but remained open as a sub-shed to Tondu until final closure on 21 December 1964. 4627 moved to Newport (Ebbw Jct)

shed in December 1962, from where it was withdrawn on 12 October 1964. It was scrapped within two months!

Top right: **NEWPORT** On the same day another pannier tank, 9616 stands in Platform 2 at Newport,, awaiting the 'right away' with a two-coach service to New Tredegar over the ex-Barry & Merthyr Railway route. The B&M line was closed north of New Tredegar in 1930, due to a landslip at the Colliery, with access to this latter then being provided by a new connection from the Rhymney Railway line at Tir Phil. New in September 1945, 9616

was just twenty years old when withdrawn – from, Severn Tunnel Jct – and rapidly scrapped.

Oppsite page: **NEW TREDEGAR** Later in the day, 9616 has arrived at its destination and has run round its train. It now stands ready for the 'off', with the signalman at the station signalbox having given the indication of a clear road by the tall ex-GWR somersault signal on the platform end, to the right of the train. The sun shines brightly and presumably the signalbox is warm, with the end window open. Note the attractive stone-faced terrace climbing the hill.

Western Region
Steam in Wales

Opposite: **NEWPORT** Three for the price of one – twice! Three roads are occupied in this busy scene on 22 September, with 'home based ' 9667 releasing pent up energy in the bay, to the right, 5099 *Compton Castle* pulling away with a down express for Swansea, centre, and a 'triple-header' in the down centre road. A trio of '2800' Class locos – 3849, 3818 and 3851 – wait for their turn for the road, to run down to the nearby Ebbw Vale engine shed.

Left: **EBBW VALE** Still in the Welsh Valleys on 22 September, we are now at the far end of the Newport-Ebbw Vale branch, looking south from Ebbw Vale station to the 1813-built archway in the bridge linking the town centre and Newtown, constructed to cater for the then new tramway. The bridge still exists in 2007. overseeing the Ebbw Vale Walk. Note the starter signals, upper left and right; a catch point protecting the left hand running line – a runaway would experience an unwelcome impact with the very solid bridge abutment!; and the two signal gantries beyond the bridge. A lonely figure lurks between the two bridges – hopefully a maintenance worker inspecting the line.

Below: **MERTHYR** The Push Pull service from Pontsticill Junction, via Cefn Coed and Pontsarn has just arrived on 7 October. The loco is '6400' Class 0-6-0PT No 6416, was turned out by the Great Western works at Swindon during November of 1934 and would remain in service until September 1963, a mere 2 years after this photograph was taken. The branch did not survive much longer!

1961 Sporting Highlights

Wimbledon

Celebrating its 75th Anniversary the singles winners were:

Rod Laver beats Chuck McKinley to win Men's Singles Final:

6-3, 6-1, 6-4

Angela Mortimer beats Christine Truman to win Women's Singles Final:

4-6, 6-4, 7-5

Phil Hill

wins the F1 Championship with Ferrari and also the Le Mans 24 Hours race

Golf

Gary Player becomes the first non-american to win the US Masters

The FA Cup 1961/2

Tottenham Hotspur win 2 - 0 against Leicester City

The League Cup 1961/2 (over two legs)

Aston Villa win after extra time

Rotherham 2 - 0 Aston Villa

Aston Villa 3 - 0 Rotherham (AET)

The Football League Champions

Tottenham Hotspur

Old Swindon Junction

Above: **SWINDON (Junction)** Your authors could not resist including this picture taken at 2.29pm one day in July 1961 as it provides background information on the year in question. *Radio Rentals* are proudly advertising a 19" square television for 10/- per month. *Radio Rentals* started life in Brighton back in 1932 doing exactly what its name suggests. Taken over first by *THORN Electrical Industries Ltd* in 1968 and later merged with *Granada*. The half cab bus was still a common sight throughout the country in 1961 and Swindon Corporation's No 56, a Park Royal bodied Daimler CVD6, is a fine example. The station building will bring back particularly strong memories for the hundreds of trainspotters who on leaving the station turned right and followed the long stone wall down to the works entrance opposite the GWR Mechanics Institute. The very lucky would have had a works visitor's pass, providing access on a given day - but for many 2pm on most Wednesday afternoon will stick in the memory, being the regular day for organised tours. *Peter Townsend collection*

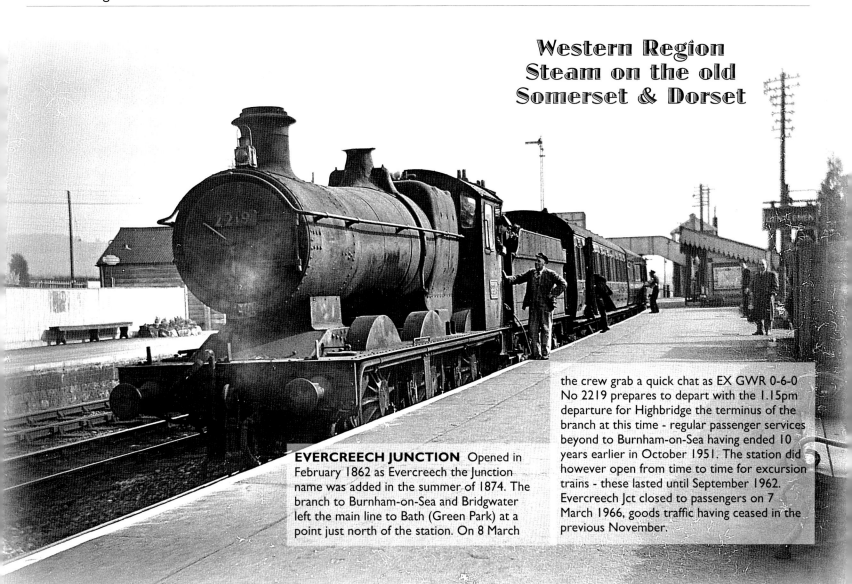

Western Region Steam on the old Somerset & Dorset

EVERCREECH JUNCTION Opened in February 1862 as Evercreech the Junction name was added in the summer of 1874. The branch to Burnham-on-Sea and Bridgwater left the main line to Bath (Green Park) at a point just north of the station. On 8 March the crew grab a quick chat as EX GWR 0-6-0 No 2219 prepares to depart with the 1.15pm departure for Highbridge the terminus of the branch at this time - regular passenger services beyond to Burnham-on-Sea having ended 10 years earlier in October 1951. The station did however open from time to time for excursion trains - these lasted until September 1962. Evercreech Jct closed to passengers on 7 March 1966, goods traffic having ceased in the previous November.

HIGHBRIDGE Seen from the footbridge the Ex-Somerset & Dorset station presents a busy scene on 8 March, No 2219 has just arrived on the 1.15pm departure from Evercreech Junction seen in the previous view and on which Ray Ruffell travelled. In the background No 3216 stands in Platform 3 with the 2.20pm to Evercreech Junction which can be seen in the picture opposite. The importance of Highbridge in these halcyon days of railways is reflected in the fact that there were no fewer than five platforms to cope with the services.

HIGHBRIDGE The old Somerset and Dorset line was still very much alive in 1961 and steam very much ruled the roost! Here we see '2251' Class 0-6-0 No 3216 in platform 3 with the 2.20pm for Evercreech Junction on 8 March. The Guard has his door open at the ready for a prompt departure. New in December 1947, the last month of the GWR, 3216 first went to Banbury. The West Midlands and South Wales then followed, before a move to Templecombe on 8 October 1960. It then worked the S&DR until withdrawal on 30 November 1963. Passenger and most goods from here to Evercreech Jct ended on 7 March 1966. Freight on the short stretch to Bason Bridge (United Dairies Sidings) survived until 2 October 1972.

Inset left: TIVERTON JUNCTION
Heading in the opposite direction, seen from the station footbridge on 16 October, also on a 'stopper' Hall Class 4-6-0 No 6965 *Thirlestaine Hall* awaits departure for Taunton

Inset right: HEMYOCK On 16 October '1400' Class 0-4-2T No 1466 (formerly No 4866) - with a steady aim into the bucket(!) - stands at the terminus of this fondly remembered branch from Tiverton Junction. The branch finally closed as late as October 1975 - the United Dairies Creamery having kept the line open for goods traffic long after the last passenger train service left on 9 September 1963. No 1466 can still be seen today having been saved from the cutters torch at the time of writing she is at *The Didcot Railway Centre.*

Above: **LEAMINGTON SPA (General)**
A place dear to your authors' (PT) heart. His Grandmother ran a cafe, restaurant and bakers in Bath Street for many years and he spent many happy hours trainspotting at both the General and Avenue stations - he lived in Swindon at the time but Coventry and Leamington became regular destinations during his school holidays! But we digress. On Friday 27 October King Class 4-6-0 No 6021 *King Richard II* is seen shortly after arrival on the 9.15am departure from Paddington. Ray Ruffell reports that the King was hauling 13 carriages and reached a speed of 85mph on the stretch from Banbury. Delivered new in June 1930 No 6021 was withdrawn less than 12 months after this shot was taken in September 1962 and was cut up during December - what a sad end for such a fine looking locomotive!

Right main picture: **TIVERTON JUNCTION**
More main line action as we find Hall Class 4-6-0 No 6914 *Langton Hall* departing from Tiverton Junction with the 12.05pm 'stopper' from Taunton going forward to Exeter on 16 October. The Hall was a well travelled engine before withdrawl from Cardiff on 13 April 1964

Western Region Steam in the Midlands, South West and London

Left: **LONDON WATERLOO** What's this - a Great Western pannier tank in the cathedral of the Southern Railway - is nothing sacred? In fact Nine Elms shed (70A) had received an allocation of GW pannier tanks during the late 1950s. '5700' Class 0-6-0PT No 9770 was one such and is seen here on an empty carriage stock working in the illustrious company of Bournemouth (71B) shed's 'West Country' Class 4-6-2 No 34043 *Combe Martin*. Prior to September 1948 this loco carried the Southern Railway No 21C143. This 6 July view makes for a wonderful contrast in design and power!

Below: **LONDON WATERLOO** Also allocated to Nine Elms - from March 1959 to July 1963 - and ECS workings '5700' Class 0-6-0PT No 4692 pulls away on 12 May from Waterloo under the watchful eye of the lookout standing flags in hand on the platform end.

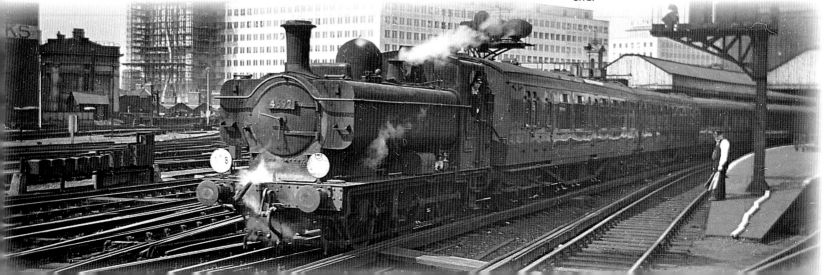

SOUTHERN RAILWAY
VENTNOR STATION
FOR SHANKLIN, SANDOWN, NEWPORT,
RYDE, PORTSMOUTH & LONDON
CHEAP TICKETS DAILY TO ALL PARTS OF THE ISLAND

500

Above: **VENTNOR** This fondly remembered station was 294ft above sea level and opened on 15 September 1866. Reached via a tunnel bored through St Boniface Down, seen here towering above the station area, the tunnel entrance can be seen beyond the signalbox in the distance.

This view taken on 12 November clearly shows the station layout, set No 500 is standing in Platform 1 which was relatively unusual on Britain's railways in that the carriages were accessible from both sides. Access to the Island Platform 2 was via a walkway that straddled the track - being

moved in place between trains. Sadly one can no longer travel by train from here to Shanklin, Sandown, Newport, Ryde, Portsmouth and London. Cheap tickets are no longer on sale as all this came to an end on 17 April 1966 to be replaced by an industrial estate.

Opposite page: **VENTNOR** This view taken at the platform end shows the tunnel mouth about to engulf the departing service for all stations to Ryde. Modellers will perhaps be interested in the intricate details of the signal gantry and the raised lettering on the station sign.

Below: **RYDE** The last remaining steam shed on the island, which had been built in 1930, closed when steam operation on the islands railways ceased with the closure of the lines from Cowes to Newport and Ryde (Smallbrook Junction) and from Shanklin to Ventnor on 17 April 1966. Seen here on 12 November 1961 looking back from the carriage window of a Ryde to Ventnor service we see no fewer than five locomotives on shed and still active on the island.

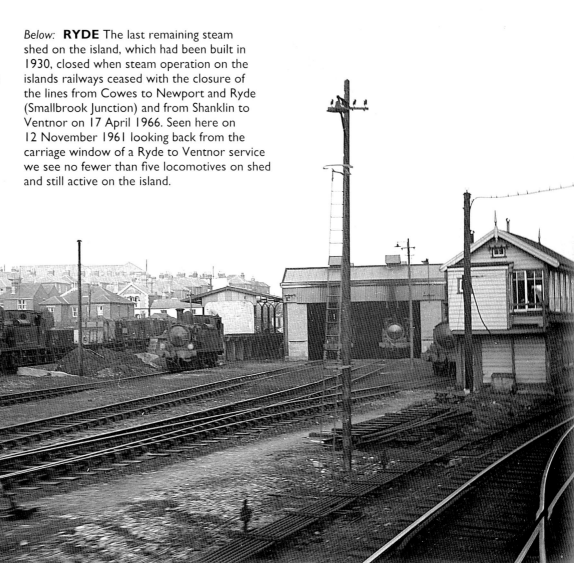

1961
Arrivals & Departures

Births

Graham Macpherson (*Suggs*)	*singer*		13 January
Andy Taylor	*singer*		16 February
Laurel Clark	*astronaut*	*(d. 2003)*	10 March
Eddie Murphy	*actor/comedian*		3 April
George Lopez	*actor/comedian*		23 April
George Clooney	*actor*		6 May
George Alan O'Dowd (Boy George)	*musician/producer*		14 June
Kalpana Chawla	*astronaut*	*(d. 2003)*	1 July
Diana Spencer	*Princess of Wales*	*(d. 1997)*	1 July
Carl Lewis	*athlete*		1 July
William C McCool	*astronaut*	*(d. 2003)*	23 September

Deaths

Morris Stanley Nichols	*English cricketer*	(b. 1900)	26 January
George Formby	*singer, actor/comedian*	(b. 1904)	6 March
Thomas Beecham	*Composer*	(b. 1879)	8 March
Gary Cooper	*actor*	(b. 1901)	13 May
Carl Jung	*psychiatrist*	(b. 1875)	6 June
Ernest Hemingway	*author*	(b. 1899)	2 July
Chico Marx	*comedian*	(b. 1887)	11 October
Earle Page	*Australian PM*	(b. 1880)	20 December

Opposite page: **RYDE PIER HEAD** This view on 12 November sees Adams 0-4-4T No 20 *Shanklin* pulling away from the buffers at Pier Head having been released by the departing service. This locomotive was built at the LSWR's Nine Elms works in 1892 and was previously numbered 30183 when working on the mainland; it was transferred to the Isle of Wight in 1923. Sadly No 20 did not survive into preservation and was withdrawn in January 1967 and scrapped in May of that year. Sister locomotive No 24 *Calbourne* faired better and is preserved on The Isle of Wight Steam Railway. At the time of writing she is nearing the completion of a major overhaul, and her return to service is eagerly awaited. For latest information visit the IOWSR web site at: www.iwsteamrailway.co.uk

Isle of Wight's railways in 1961

Lines open ———
Lines closed – – –

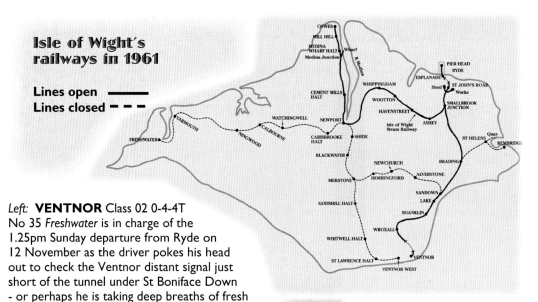

Left: **VENTNOR** Class 02 0-4-4T No 35 *Freshwater* is in charge of the 1.25pm Sunday departure from Ryde on 12 November as the driver pokes his head out to check the Ventnor distant signal just short of the tunnel under St Boniface Down - or perhaps he is taking deep breaths of fresh air prior to entering the smokey atmosphere inside the tunnel! No 35 was built way back in may 1890 at the LSWR's Nine Elms Works. She originally carried the number 30181 before being sent to the island in 1949. She was withdrawn in October 1966 and scrapped in May 1967

Right: **RYDE PIER HEAD** Here we see the same train awaiting departure from Pier Head station, the fireman having made sure the tanks are full ready for the journey to Ventnor, a distance of some 12½ miles. Ex London Transport tube stock now run the service from here as far as Shanklin.

Farewell to two old-timers!

30287

Above: **EASTLEIGH Shed** T9 Class 4-4-0 No 30287 was built in January 1900 and officially withdrawn in September 1961 but is seen here on the scrap road on 24 July looking very unlikely to move under her own steam again! In fact she went to the torch in November 1961. She had been based at Fratton (FRA) at nationalisation in 1948 but moved to Eastleigh shed shortly after.

Below left: **EASTLEIGH Shed** Adams 4-4-2T No 30584 is seen on the scrap road on 24 July. She had been withdrawn from duties on the Lyme Regis branch in February and would languish here until the end finally came in December. She was one of just three of the class of seventy one examples built between 1882 and 1885 to survive into British Railways ownership. They were retained to run the Lyme Regis branch services and were officially based at Salisbury shed. The other two locos were Nos 30582 and 30583. At the time of writing No 30583 the only survivor is awaiting major overhaul at *The Bluebell Railway*.

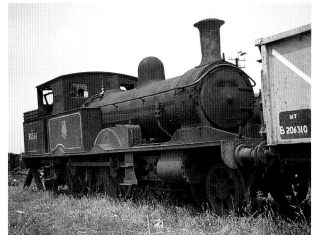

1961
TV Favourites
a selection

Ask Mr Pastry (BBC)
Childrens Sitcom starring Richard Hearne as Mr Pastry & Dandy Nichols as Mrs Spindle
Comedy Playhouse (BBC)
The first of over 100 half hour sitcoms
Bootsie and Snudge (Granada)
A spin off from the *The Army Game* (BBC) featuring the demobbed characters played by Alfie Bass and Bill Fraser
The Morcambe and Wise Show (ATV)
The start of the legendary shows starring Eric and Ernie
The Rag Trade (BBC)
Fenner Fashions first hit the screen in 1961 starring Reg Varney, Peter Jones and Miriam Karlin and rapidly became a must see sitcom for thousands of viewers
The Avengers (ABC)
The detective series that starred Ian Hendry as *Dr David Keel* and Patrick Macnee as *John Steed* in the first series and which went on to star Honor Blackman as *Cathy Gale* and Diana Rigg as *Emma Peel*
Coronation Street (Granada)
Should need no introduction, but having started in 1960 as a regional programme the legendry show went national in '61

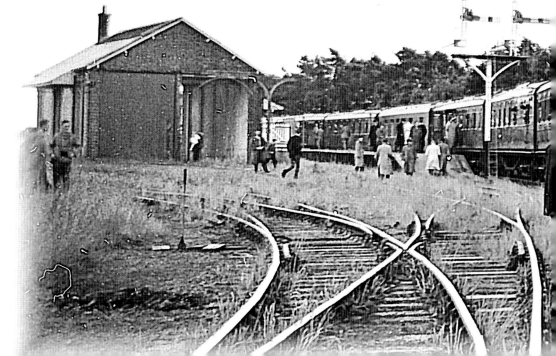

locomotive was one of a total of 109, Harry Wainwright designed, examples built for the South Eastern and Chatham Railway (SECR) between 1900 and 1908. Withdrawn just four months after this duty, this loco was to be saved from the scrap yard that beckoned all the other members of the class, and is now based at *The Bluebell Railway*. At the time of writing the locomotive is undergoing a major overhaul in preparation for a further return to steam.

Main picture: **HAWKHURST** A marvellous, but of course sad, view of Hawkhurst as the last train proves too long to fit into the platforms! There are people everywhere determined to give the station area a final but detailed inspection. The goods shed and the roads leading to it are already being taken over by nature. The signal gantry looks to be in remarkable condition having presumably been repainted along with the previously seen signalbox in recent times. The crew of 01 Class 0-6-0 No 31065 wait patiently for the second train loco No 31592 to complete its run round manoeuvre. Happily No 31065 also survived the cutters torch and is also beautifully restored and based on *The Bluebell Railway*.

Above: **HAWKHURST** On Sunday 11 June 'C' Class 0-6-0 No 31592 runs round the special passing the well maintained, if a little leaning, signalbox and water tower. It is hard to imagine that this was to be the last train to Hawkhust save for the demolition train! This

ON TOUR
LCGB The South Eastern Limited

11th June 1961
L.C.G.B.
The South Eastern Limited
Source of route and timings data:
http://www.sixbellsjunction.co.uk
Terry Jackson & Trevor Machell

Loco(s)	Route
31749 + 31786	London Victoria - Stewarts Lane Jn - Factory Jn - Wandsworth Road - Brixton - Nunhead - Lewisham - Blackheath - Bexleyheath - Dartford - Gravesend - Strood - Snodland - Maidstone West - Paddock Wood
31065 + 31592	Paddock Wood - Hawkhurst
31065 + 31592	Hawkhurst - Paddock Wood - Tonbridge
31308 + 31749	Tonbridge - Tunbridge Wells Central - Robertsbridge
32662 + 32670	Robertsbridge - Tenterden
32662 + 32670	Tenterden - Robertsbridge
31786 + 31749	Robertsbridge - Tunbridge Wells Central - Tonbridge - Sevenoaks - Otford - Swanley - Beckenham Junction - New Beckenham - Ladywell - Parks Bridge Jn - St Johns - London Charing Cross

Locos Used: 31065, 31308, 31592, 31749, 31786, 32662 & 32670
Stock Used: 9 Carriages (7 advertised but 2 more added for part of trip)

Above: **TENTERDEN** 'Terriers' Nos 32670 and 32662 'top and tailed' the train from Robertsbridge to Tenterden and return. Here we see the former with much adulation from the travellers and the local populace who turned out to see what they thought would be the last train to call here.

Left: **ROBERTSBRIDGE** 'H' Class 0-4-4T No 31308 and '01' Class 4-4-0 No 31749, of Tonbridge and Bricklayers Arms sheds respectively, having taken over the train at Tonbridge for the journey to Robertsbridge via Tunbridge Wells Central, are seen on arrival at Robertsbridge. Ray records on the back of the original photograph that a speed of 74mph was attained by the double header on route to Robertsbridge!

Below: **TENTERDEN** The special arrives at Tenterden behind Terrier Loco No 32662 and a mass exodus ensues. This was thought to be 'The Last Train' as the line was closed and due for demolition. However a 13 year struggle by enthusiasts resulted in Tenterden being saved along with the line back as far as Bodiam. The Kent and East Sussex Railway is now a thriving preserved line and readers are encouraged to pay them a visit!

Opposite left: **BODIAM** Close inspection of the fence post is made as the special arrives at the now preserved terminus of Bodiam behind Terrier No 32662 and looking rather like an elephant with tusks!

Opposite right: **GOUDHURST** '01' Class 0-6-0 No 31065 and behind her 'C' Class 0-6-0 No 31592 are captured by the camera at Goudhurst on the last train to Hawkhurst. Note the limited space for photographers.

M.C	Location	Booked
0.00	Victoria	09.52d
1.37	Stewarts Lane Jn	09/57
1.73	Factory Jn	10*02a ~ 10*06d
3.18	Brixton	10/10
3.72	Cambria Jn	10/11½
5.78	Nunhead	10/15
7.63	Lewisham	10/23½
8.55	Blackheath	10/26
10.61	Eltham Well Hall	10p32a ~ 10p37d
14.39	Bexleyheath	10/44
18.60	Dartford	10/53
25.44	Gravesend Central	11*07a ~ 11*10d
32.60	Strood	11/22
44.05	Maidstone West	11/42
48.69	Wateringbury	11p52a ~ 12p01d
54.01	Paddock Wood	12.12a ~ 12.22d
58.30	Horsmonden	12p32a ~ 12p42d
60.31	Goudhurst	12p48a ~ 12p58d
63.77	Cranbrook	13p07a ~ 13p15d
65.38	Hawkhurst	13.20a ~ 13.35d
76.75	Paddock Wood	14/00
82.18	Tonbridge	14.08a ~ 14.21d
87.07	Tunbridge Wells Central	14/33
92.00	Wadhurst	14/41
102.25	Robertsbridge	14.56a ~ 15.10d
105.60	Bodiam	15p23a ~ 15p32d
109.25	Northiam	15p39a ~ 15p48d
111.55	Wittersham Road	15p55a ~ 16p05d
114.31	Rolvendon	16p13a ~ 16p23d
115.65	Tenterden Town	16.30a ~ 16.55d
117.19	Rolvenden	17p00a ~ 17p10d
119.75	Wittersham Road	17*17a ~ 17*20d
122.25	Northiam	17/29
125.70	Bodiam	17/39
129.25	Robertsbridge	17.55a ~ 18.10d
139.50	Wadhurst	18/24
144.42	Tunbridge Wells Central	18/32
149.32	Tonbridge	18/40
156.67	Sevenoaks	18/54
159.47	Otford	18/59
166.22	Swanley	19/09
171.29	Bickley Jn	19/15
173.68	Shortlands	19/19
175.01	Beckenham Junction	19/21
175.52	New Beckenham	19/25
177.54	Catford Bridge	19/28
178.71	Parks Bridge Jn	19/31
180.16	New Cross	19/33
183.15	London Bridge	19/38
183.53	Metropolitan Jn	19/40
185.04	Charing Cross	19.44a

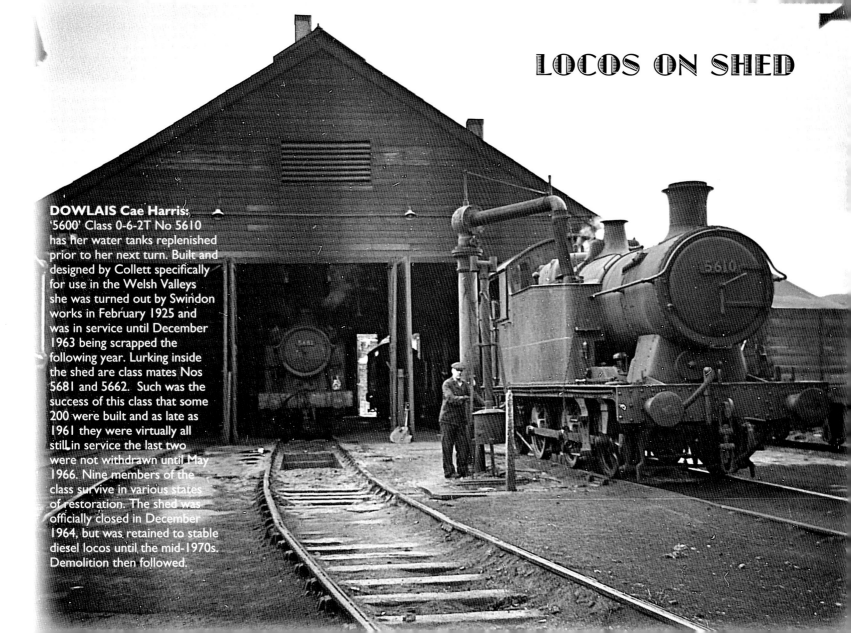

DOWLAIS Cae Harris: '5600' Class 0-6-2T No 5610 has her water tanks replenished prior to her next turn. Built and designed by Collett specifically for use in the Welsh Valleys she was turned out by Swindon works in February 1925 and was in service until December 1963 being scrapped the following year. Lurking inside the shed are class mates Nos 5681 and 5662. Such was the success of this class that some 200 were built and as late as 1961 they were virtually all still in service the last two were not withdrawn until May 1966. Nine members of the class survive in various states of restoration. The shed was officially closed in December 1964, but was retained to stable diesel locos until the mid-1970s. Demolition then followed.

Below: **BOURNEMOUTH Shed (71B)** 'M7' Class 0-4-4T No 30127 is seen here on the turntable road - a distinct lack of buffer stops would seem to be asking for trouble, certainly would have focused the drivers concentration! This loco spent time at Salisbury, Eastleigh and Bournemouth sheds post-nationalisation and was withdrawn in November 1963 and scrapped the same month.

Right: **SALISBURY** This photograph is without details in Ray's files, but is thought to be Salisbury shed, where ex-GWR locomotives were frequent visitors to Southern metals.

To the left, 5376 appears to be receiving some form of attention and, allocated to Bristol (St Philips Marsh) shed, it has no doubt worked into the Salisbury area on a duty from Bristol. To its right, 30502 is a visitor from London, allocated to Feltham and bearing the disc code representing a train bound for Salisbury and/or Portsmouth Harbour via Eastleigh. Its companion is BR 'Standard' 73118 *King Leodegrance*, with a headcode signifying a service to Southampton terminus and/or Portsmouth Harbour. The quartet is completed by an unidentified WR 'Hall'. Note the proliferation of smoke and steam!

This page: **BANFF** BR Standard Class '2' 2-6-0 No 78054 awaits its 2.30pm departure time. The driver is sporting the 'mandatory grease cap' with the British Railways badge which was produced in different colours for each of the regions. Being Scotland this one would have been light blue with nickel lettering. The single road loco shed, which closed on 7 July 1964, is seen in the background. 78054 was new in December 1955, to Motherwell, moving north to Aberdeen ten months later. Its northern sojourn then lasted until July 1964,

when it moved to Bathgate, southwest of Edinburgh, from where the end came officially on Christmas Day 1965 - when just ten years old!

Opposite page: **BANFF** The same train looking in the opposite direction shows the pleasing station building complete with all over roof. This line opened in July 1859 and closed to passengers on 6 July 1964. Freight services to Banff lingered on until complete closure in May 1968.

1961
Happenings (1)

January
- The millionth Morris Minor produced
- Elsa the lioness made famous through Joy Adamson's book *Born Free* dies
- The Birth Control Pill sold in Britain's pharmacies for the first time
- *101 Dalmations* one of the all time classics from Walt Disney is released in the US

February
- Airliner crashes in Belgium all 18 members of the US World Figure Skating Team lose their lives
- Initial plans for London's Post Office Tower are released
- New York hit by blizzards - with over 16 inches of snow reported

March
- George Formby the popular singer, comedian and musician passed away
- Dr Richard Beeching takes up his post as head of British Railways

April
- Yuri Gagarin of Russia becomes the first man in space
- Britain applies for membership of the European Economic Community
- Judy Garland returns after illness to perform at New York's Carnegie Hall to wide acclaim

ON SCOTTISH LINES

Inset: **BEITH TOWN** This line closed to passengers on 5 November 1962 and as can be seen passengers in latter days were scarce and the Wickham Railbus No SC79965 was more than adequate by this late stage in the lines life. The picture taken on 1 December, shows that gas lighting was still the order of the day! The train is the 12.40 pm departure to Lugton.

Main picture: **DUNPHAIL (between Forres and Aviemore)** On 9 August smoke trails back from 'Class 5' 4-6-0 No 45470 working hard with the Edinburgh and Glasgow service which departed from Inverness at 9.50 am that dull and cloudy morning. A Perth engine for much of its BR life - and working from that shed at the date of this view - it would have known this route intimately. Moving to the Glasgow area in April 1962, it was withdrawn in September 1964.

Below: **NAIRN** On 6 August the signalman has left his box to exchange the tablet with the leading driver of the Edinburgh - Perth - Inverness express as it rattles through Nairn. This service carried a restaurant car and was double headed by two 'Type 2' Sulzer locomotives. The footbridge, station building and both East and West signalboxes are protected listed buildings and can still be enjoyed today.

Right: **NAIRN** It is now 8 August and we have crossed over the footbridge and a stopping train has arrived behind 'Class 5' 4-6-0 No 45496. This 'Black Five', as members of the Class were/are commonly known, is just one of 842 built between 1934 and 1951. Not surprisingly the 'Black Fives' were amongst the very last steam locomotives to be in service with British Railways during August 1968. No 45496, however, succumbed to the inevitable on 27 June 1964.

Main picture: **LOCH CARRON** On 14 August 1961 this was the view from the Ex-Devon Belle observation car attached to the 9.15am departure from Inverness on route to Kyle of Lochalsh. In October 2006 there is still a 9.15am departure from Inverness but this *First Scot Rail* service runs only as far as Dingwall, the equivalent through service to Kyle leaving at 8.53am and arriving at 11.20am.

Inset below: **KYLE OF LOCHALSH** 14 August was a very wet day as can be seen from this view of the terminus taken from the road above the station, I thought readers might like to see a comparative view, *(Inset right)* not

August 2006

quite from the same angle but hopefully a fascinating comparison none the less - some things never change, the weather!

Inset right upper: **KYLE OF LOCHALSH** Back to 1961 and Sulzer 'Type 2' D5337 having arrived with the 9.15am from Inverness on 14 August now runs round the train and onwards to the loco depot for servicing, whilst the passengers hurry from the rain!

Inset below: **KYLE OF LOCHALSH SHED** Later in the day Ray captured D5323 on the left with the observation car to be attached, for the return working, to the incoming 1.53pm from Inverness which is seen approaching on the right double headed by two further unidentified Type 2s.

1961
Happenings (2)

May
- Alan Shepard becomes first American in space just a month after the Russians
- Formation of Coventry, Colchester and Canterbury Universities announced
- Gary Cooper the double *Oscar* winning actor dies of cancer
- George Blake found guilty of Spying and sentanced to 42 years in prison

June
- Dr Michael Ramsey becomes the 100th Archbishop of Canterbury he will be the first Archbishop of Canterbury to visit Rome for an audience with the Pope
- Rudolf Nureyev defects in Paris while on tour with the Kirov Ballet Company

July
- British troops land in Kuwait due to the threat of invasion by Iraq
- Ernest Hemingway best selling author commits suicide

August
- Construction of the Berlin Wall starts, many East Germans flee to the West before the border is sealed
- The A6 murder commited - becomes the subject of long running appeal on behalf of James Hanratty against his conviction

Opposite: **THURSO** Right up in the far north of Scotland is the terminus at Thurso. This is the view on 11 August taken from the road bridge south of the station. This would make a good choice for a railway modeller, having a compact but interesting four road goods yard and loco shed on the right, plus a bay platform on the left.

Below: **FRASERBURGH** A busy freight yard existed here, as can be seen on the right, and services ran to Aberdeen via Maud Junction on the main line and a branch line ran to St. Combs. On 15 August the St Combs railcar can be seen in the platform road and the home starter signal shows departure is imminent. Sadly the branch closed in May 1964 and all passenger services to Fraserburgh ceased in October 1965. Goods traffic however continued for several more years but closure to all traffic came in October 1979.

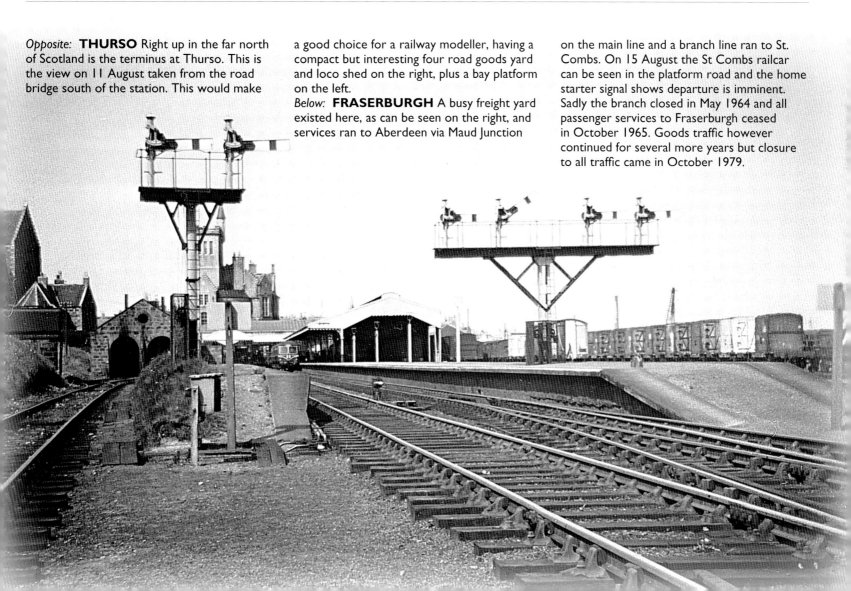

MAUD JUNCTION How could we throw all this away? The lines in the centre are the 'main lines' to Fraserburgh, while on the right are what were the main lines until the late 1940s heading off to Peterhead. This view was taken from the front cab of the 12.22pm departure from Aberdeen on 15 August. The train was stopped short of the station to allow the rear two carriages to be detached to form the onward service to Peterhead while the main train would continue to Fraserburgh. Approaching on the right from Peterhead is North British 'Type 2' D6140 in charge of a freight service. This is of course all gone,

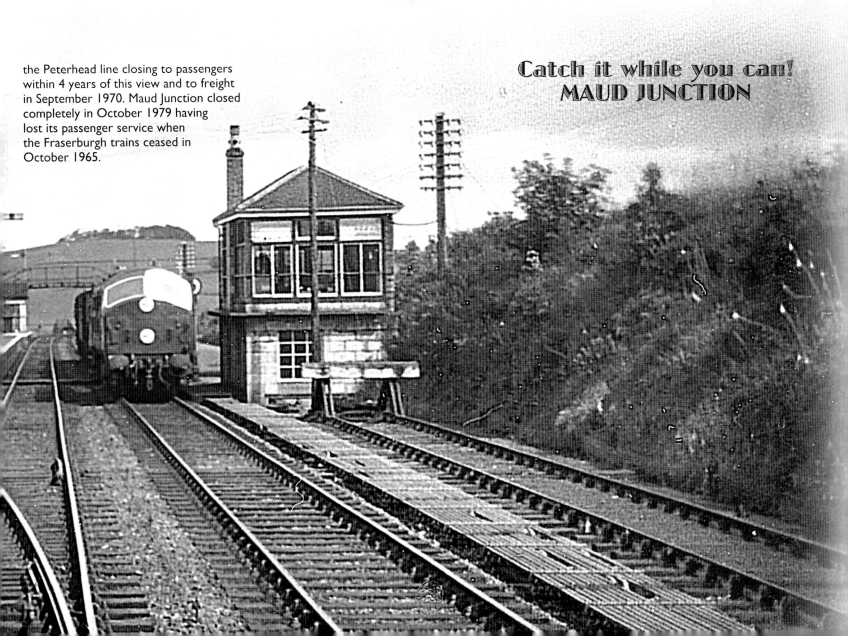

the Peterhead line closing to passengers within 4 years of this view and to freight in September 1970. Maud Junction closed completely in October 1979 having lost its passenger service when the Fraserburgh trains ceased in October 1965.

Catch it while you can!
MAUD JUNCTION

1961
No 1 Records

January
I love you	*Cliff Richards*
Poetry in motion	*Johnny Tillotson*
Are you lonesome tonight	*Elvis Presley*

February
Sailor	*Petula Clarke*

March
Walk right back	*The Everly Brothers*
Wooden heart	*Elvis Presley*

April

Wooden heart - *stays at No 1*

May
Blue moon	*The Marcels*
On the rebound	*Floyd Cramer*
You're driving me crazy	*The Temperance Seven*

June
Surrender	*Elvis Presley*
Runaway	*Del Shannon*

July
Temptation	*The Everly Brothers*

August
Well I ask you	*Eden Kane*
You don't know	*Helen Shapiro*
Johnny remember me	*John Leyton*

September

Reach for the stars / Climb every mountain *Shirley Bassey*

October
Kon Tiki	*The Shadows*
Michael	*The Highwaymen*
Walkin' back to happiness	*Helen Shapiro*

November
His latest flame	*Elvis Presley*

December
Tower of strength	*Frankie Vaughan*
Moon River	*Danny Williams*

Express Steam
Midland & Scottish Region

Below: **PERTH** On 17 August 'Coronation' Class 4-6-2 No 46237 *City of Bristol* awaits departure with the 12.20pm Express for London Euston while pulling away alongside is 'A4' Class 4-6-2 No 60027 *Merlin*. These 'Titans of the steel highway' were both designed for the London to Scotland Express services. The LNER built the 'A4' in 1937 for services on the East Coast route and the LMS turned out the Coronation in 1939 for their West Coast route. *Merlin* (withdrawn 1965) lasted longer than the *City of Bristol* (withdrawn 1964)

Above: **LONDON EUSTON** 'Princess' Class 4-6-2 No 46200 *The Princess Royal* has a good head of steam evidenced by the safety valves blowing off as she awaits her next roster. The fireman takes time out to see what is happening in the world outside the footplate. Built at Crewe in 1933 *The Princess Royal* was withdrawn in November 1962 but not scrapped until October 1964. Sadly during this long period of inactivity the preservationist did not come to this fine locomotives rescue. Thankfully sister locomotives No 46201 *Princess Elizabeth* and No 46203 *Princess Margaret Rose* were saved for the enjoyment of future generations.

Opposite page: **LONDON EUSTON** Driver A. Stobbs and Fireman J. Horsfield are clearly happy in their work and today Saturday 30 June they are going to take the 10.35 am service to Carlisle behind 'Coronation' Class 4-6-2 No 46220 *Coronation*. On arrival at Carlisle they will be signing off duty at their home shed Carlisle Upperby (12B)

1961
Happenings (3)

September
- Sierra Leone admitted to the United Nations
- NASA announces that the new Lyndon B Johnson Space Centre would be established in Houston Texas

October
- The last steam hauled passenger train runs on the London Underground
- Malta gains independence from Britain
- The Ten Shilling note is reduced in size

November
- Stalingrad renamed Volgograd as part of Khrushchev's de-Stalinization policy
- Joseph Heller's *Catch 22* first published
- U Thant elected acting Secretary General of The United Nations

December
- First US troops land by helicopter in Vietnam signalling the start of the Vietnam war
- Israel finds Adolf Eichman guilty of crimes against humanity for his part in the Holocaust

Above: **LONDON EUSTON** Please do not leave your bags unattended! Back in 1961 it was all so different - or perhaps the gentleman with his arms folded is the owner of the bag... 'Coronation' Class 4-6-2 No 46220 *Coronation*, seen in the previous picture on page 42, is here viewed from the adjacent platform. The power of these front line ex-LMS locomotives can be fully appreciated at this distance. Outshopped from Crewe in June 1937 this locomotive briefly held the world speed record for a steam locomotive having attained a speed of 114 mph on Tuesday 29 June 1937 in the very capable hands of Crewe driver Tom Clarke. Having driven the Royal Train from Crewe, Tom was awarded the OBE in recognition of this achievement by King George VI on 12 July 1937 on arrival at Euston. Tom was still wearing his overalls! *Virgin Trains* named 'Class 90' locomotive 90014, *Driver Tom Clark O.B.E.* on 16 June 2002. The nameplate has since been transferred to 'Class 47' Loco No 47832, being applied on 11 September 2005.

The Whiskers are growing!

below: **RHYMNEY** A Gloucester C & W built 'Class 119' DMU awaits departure from this head of valleys station for Cardiff (Queen Street). Looking north towards Rhymney Bridge the waiting room can be seen to the left of the DMU along with a grounded coach body thought to be an original RR carriage dating back to the late 1800s. Note the call starter signal and the anti slip ridges on the platform end slope. The delights of Guernsey are extolled on the hoarding above the buffer stops - quite a hike from here!

Above: **EBBW VALE** The day is a dull 22 September and the three-car set stands at Ebbw Vale (Low Level), waiting for the relatively short trip to Aberbeeg. The BR Derby Works 'Class 116' set has DMBS 50085 leading. New in August 1957, it saw less than 20 years service, for, whilst its companions largely survived until the late-1980s-mid-1990s, being renumbered along the way, 50085 was withdrawn in July 1975, still with its original number. It was cut up by the Bird Group at Lichfield Station. Note the parcels awaiting attention and the signalbox on the platform beyond.

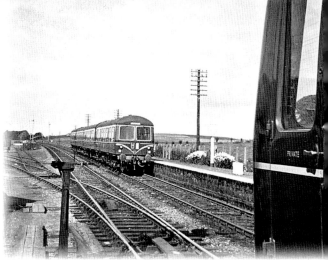

Above left: **ST COMBS** On 15 August the driver is changing the destination blind of Cravens DMU Class 105 DMBS SC51475 as it awaits departure time. Built in February 1959, it is still fairly new and no doubt the guard is happy to collect fares in this relative comfort. Withdrawn in November 1981, it was torched, quite literally, by A King's yard at Snailwell, in Suffolk. The blind shows Boat of Garten but this is merely a snapshot in time, as the driver will wind on to show Fraserburgh. The service also called at Cairnbulg (this halt having previously been known as Inverallochy after the other hamlet nearby), Philorth Bridge and Kirkton Bridge. The branch closed in 1964 and the station site is now beneath a housing development.

Above right: **AUCHNAGATT** More Cravens 105s on show, this time crossing in the station confines. At approximately 12.20 p.m., approaching is the service from Fraserburgh and Peterhead. Both made up of two cars, they had joined forces at Maud Jct before continuing their journey south. Just visible to the right, is the mirror service in the opposite direction, to be the 12.22 p.m. departure.

Bottom left: **BLAENAVON (Low Level)** The destination blind on the 'Class 119' DMU reads Brynmawr via Newport which if correct is an awfully circuitous and long journey. Terminus of the erstwhile Great Western branch from Pontnewynydd, the station shown here opened in 1854, with 'Low Level' being added in 1950. It closed in 1962 in common with most of the branch.

The Whiskers are growing

Top right: **NEW HOLLAND PIER** An unidentified 2 car DMU stands awaiting departure on Friday 15 December. The new Humber Bridge signalled the death knell of this service which ended in 1981 after 133 years service to those wishing to visit Kingston-upon-Hull on the other side of the Humber. *Inset* Paddle Steamer *Wingfield Castle* built for the LNER and launched in 1934 is seen at the pier on the same day. She made her last ferry crossing on 14 May 1974, but can still be seen today at Hartlepool Museum's Historic Dockyard.

Bottom Right: **MILDENHALL** On 7 September Railbus No E79961 stands at the terminus of this fenland branch which ran to a junction at Fordham and Burwell on the Ely to Newmarket line. The branch closed to passengers in 1962 and to all traffic in 1964. Driver W. Barham keeps a watchful eye on the photographer. Behind him on the station wall is the branch time table and on the left a poster proclaiming the benefits of Clacton-on-Sea, still a popular destination by rail in these last days before the branch succumbed to the motor car. New in April 1958, it was withdrawn in February 1967 and cut up at Slag Reduction, Ickles in the same month, the only one of the type NOT to be preserved !

Index

Acknowledgements - or those who helped oil the wheels!

First and foremost we would like to record our gratitude to the late Ray Ruffell without whom this book would not have been possible. Ray was a railwayman through and through and his interest went far beyond his day to day work, extending from miniature railways through narrow gauge to the most obscure industrial railways. Ray travelled the length and breadth of the British Isles and many locations abroad in pursuit of his subject.

Thankfully for us, and indeed future generations, Ray was also an accomplished photographer. His extensive collection has been kept complete and forms an important part of the photographic archives of The NOSTALGIA Collection.

By way of representing our gratitude to all who have helped and/or supported, here are just a few names...
Frances Townsend for sustaining her husband through the process; and Brian Morrison - a great supporter of Silver Link over many years - for his fund of knowledge on all things DMU and much more besides. Thanks are due to Gary Thornton and his contributors to the excellent web site Six Bells Junction, a mine of information on rail tours and more (http://www.sixbellsjunction.co.uk/).

So many people have helped - with snippets and guidance, facts and information - space, and space alone, precludes mention of them all, so THANK YOU ALL!